Th

Flight …*spatcher*

A Simplified, Scenario-based Training Program

Arman Rezaee

Jan 2022

Edited by: Sarah Jantz, Angelita Flores
Technical Review: Tim Antolovic, Sarah Baker
Cover Design: Reyhan Bakhoda
www.ReyhanBakhoda.com

ISBN: 9798401788139

Acknowledgment

Special thanks to Sarah Baker, David June and Frank Coppola who shared their ideas on the topics of this book and also did a fantastic job with the technical proofreading of this book.

I am grateful for *Tim Antolovic* who spent hours out of his busy schedule to read this book for compliance.

This book would have never sounded and read naturally without the amazing editing job of *Sarah Jantz* and *Angelita Flores*. For that I am very grateful.

And last but by no means least, *Reyhaneh Bakhoda*, the greatest cover designer I could ever imagine.

During the years I have had the honor to learn many of the things mentioned in this book from the following colleagues. In no specific order:

Craig Marquis ,Greg Hajdyla, Steve Olson, Scott Ramsey, Pete Zimmerman, Bill Sherrod, Carlos Jimenez and all my fellow sector managers

Intentionally Left Blank

Contents

Abbreviations & Acronyms

ACARS: *Aircraft Communications Addressing and Reporting System*

AMS: *Amsterdam Airport Schiphol - Netherlands*

ATC: *Air Traffic Control*

BOS: *Boston Logan International Airport*

CBP: U.S. *Customs and Border Protection*

CDR: *Coded Departure Routes*

CLT: *Charlotte Douglas International Airport*

COVID: *Coronavirus*

DCA: *Ronald Reagan Washington National Airport, Arlington VA*

DRM: *Dispatch Resource Management*

EDCT: *Estimated Departure Clearance Time*

ETA: *Estimated Time of Arrival*

ETD: *Estimated Time of Departure*

ETR: *Estimated Time of Repair*

GDP: *Ground Delay Program*

GS: *Ground Stop*

JFK: *John F. Kennedy International Airport (New York)*

KEF: *Keflavik Airport in Iceland*

LAS: *Las Vegas McCarran International Airport*

LGA: *LaGuardia Airport (Queens, New York)*

LHR: *London Heathrow Airport (United Kingdom)*

MEL: *Minimum Equipment List*

MIT: *Miles-in-Trail*

MOGT: *Minimum Objective Ground Time*

NOTAM: *Notification to Airmen*

OTS: *Out of Service*

PHL: *Philadelphia International Airport*

PHX: *Phoenix Sky Harbor International Airport, Phoenix Arizona*

RNO: *Reno-Tahoe International Airport*

RON: *Remain Over Night (when -ing is added, it refers to the action of remaining overnight)*

SAN: *San Diego International Airport*

SWAP: *Severe Weather Avoidance Plan*

TBFM: *Time-Based Flow Management*

US: *United States of America*

W&BD: *Weight & Balance Department*

WX: *Weather*

Preface

Starting a new technical career in aviation is both very exciting and extremely rewarding. One of the most time and money-efficient means of obtaining an FAA Airman Certificate is by obtaining a Flight Dispatcher License. If you'd like to have a career that never gets boring and pays really well, the job of a Flight Dispatcher is the way to go.·

The Flight Dispatcher License is a requirement to dispatch a flight and it usually takes around 5-6 weeks of training to obtain it. (If you study hard and are committed to it, of course).
There are plenty of high-level Flight dispatch schools around the world that teach you how to obtain your license during their training period (Next Page picture – Box 1).

Box 1 mainly focuses on teaching you the regulations and FAA requirements of being a Flight Dispatcher. They also focus on teaching you how to do flight performance calculations, flight planning, reading weather information and so on.

On the other end of this spectrum (Box 3) is when you're finally hired by your airline of choice and start airline specific training with them. Depending on your previous experience in the airline industry (and as a flight dispatcher specifically), your airline-specific training can take from 1 to 6 months.

Box 3 phase is focused on teaching you all company policies, aircraft specific systems and performance and so on.

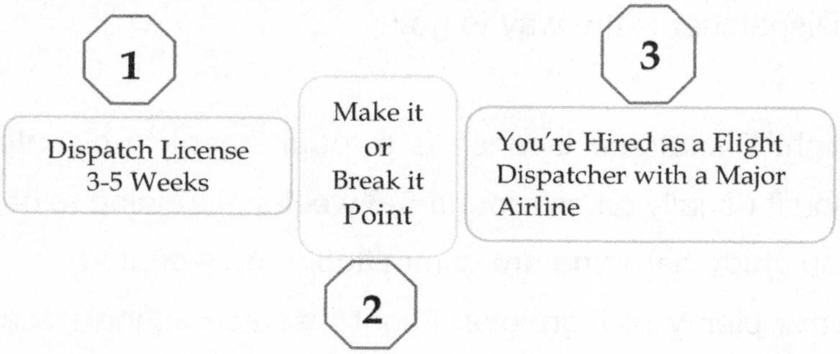

The focus of this book however, is on Box 2 section where you as a licensed flight dispatcher expand on your skill sets and knowledge to increase your hire-ability chances. And if you are already working for a domestic Part 121 or Part 135 operations, it will help you build muscle memory on how to think and decide like a seasoned major airline flight dispatcher. Box 2 section is the gap between your formal training to obtain your FAA Flight Dispatcher License and to get hired as a flight dispatcher with a major Part 121 airline.

This is where I would like to focus and help you develop a solid foundation to increase your chances of becoming the next generation of flight dispatchers for major airlines and contribute to the safety of flights.

This book is not designed to help you obtain your Flight Dispatch License. Nor does it contain any technical or regulatory information. However, by developing a solid understanding of how the airline business of major carriers operate, you will significantly improve your chances of acing your next in-person and scenario-based airline dispatcher job interview.

Furthermore, if you have already dispatched in a domestic regional airline, this book and its scenarios will help you complete your airline-specific Training (Box 3) much faster and get signed off earlier than anticipated.

What this book, along with my other book "50+ Skills that Make Your Life Easier As a Flight Dispatcher" tend to do is to help you learn and expand on the skills that usually take many years for new dispatchers to develop through experience and many hours of flight dispatching.

The scenarios chosen for this book are some of the most common challenges dispatch operations go through on a regular and day-to-day basis.

I highly recommend creating a mental checklist for yourself when reading through each chapter and try to have a bigger picture in mind in each and every scenario.

Try to think about all flights that will be impacted in that scenario and not only your flight. Always think and see the big picture.

For example, during a major weather event, if you only focus and care about your own 5 flights that are diverting to your alternate airport, you will end up in the same place that all other dispatchers ended up. In other words, your flights will divert to the same airports as other dispatcher's flights.

You have got to get creative, think outside-of-the-box and think a few steps ahead. Try to practice the what-ifs in each scenario and if you don't know the answers, ask your instructors, your friends who work as a flight dispatcher and so on. Don't let any of your what-ifs go unanswered.

We are planning on having an in-person and digital course to expand more on these scenarios and much more.

Stay tuned on YouTube and social media to learn about upcoming classes.

Thank you for reading this book.

Why Scenario-Based Training?

There are many reasons why this methodology was chosen to explain advanced flight dispatch challenging events.

Real Life Events

The events chosen in this book are some of the most common events occurring on a daily basis at larger legacy airlines in the U.S. and in the world. Having a real-life event as a reference allows us to expand and explain the steps that we possibly could/could not take to handle a certain situation.

Safety Comes First

Using a scenario-based event is our opportunity to emphasize on the importance of safety in every decision a flight dispatcher makes. Safety should be a flight dispatcher's number one priority. An unsafe decision has no place in today's airline operation.

Easier to Comprehend and Connect

It makes it easier for the reader to relate to the scenario and build muscle memory as they follow through the events step-by-step. There are numerous studies that confirm readers connect to a real event much more than reading generic instructions.

What Does This Book Teach / Not Teach You?

We recommend you study this book after you receive your initial Flight Dispatch training and/or after you obtain your Flight Dispatch License.

The topics presented in this book are chosen to benefit those who are getting ready to make the move from a small regional airline into a larger legacy carrier with a larger fleet of airplanes and many international destinations in different parts of the globe.

This book can also benefit those with a flight dispatcher license who are preparing for their oral part of their airline flight dispatch job interview where scenario-based questions are being asked.

This book does NOT teach you how to dispatch a flight. In order to obtain your flight dispatcher license, you should contact a flight dispatch school near you to receive more information on how to obtain your license.

This book does NOT supersede your current or future airline's training program. You should always follow the policies and procedures required by your company and the FAA to dispatch a flight.

This book is an experience-based manual to lay out the bigger picture and describes the important areas you, as a flight dispatcher need to consider for your planning purposes.

Intentionally Left Blank

SCENARIO 1

Late International (Non-Pre-Cleared Station) Departure to a Station with Limited CBP Hours

This is one of those scenarios that requires a ton of collaboration and coordination to make it work. When departing a non-pre cleared station, it means the international departure station doesn't have any U.S. customs to clear your customers to enter to the U.S. Customers will then need to clear customs inspections once they arrive in the U.S.

Pre-COVID (Before 2020), clearing customs usually wasn't an issue for incoming international flights to the U.S.

With COVID situation, due to decrease in air travel demand, CBP was only committed to limited hours of operation.

Let's pick a flight from KEF to JFK as an example.

CBP operating hours in JFK are set from 0800 to 2100 daily. (Not actual hours)

Our flight from KEF airport has been delayed due to a mechanical problem. Considering the time that it takes to address the mechanical issue, complete the maintenance logbooks and so forth, the estimated time of arrival (ETA) is set to 2300.

This is clearly outside of CBP's operating hours in our JFK station. Disregarding these hours (intentionally or unintentionally) will bring your airline a very hefty fine as it is clearly a violation of CBP and company dispatch policies.

You have a few options here:

To Stop and Clear Customs in the Third Airport

This is your best option (most of the time) and that is to find a station that has a longer CBP hours or ideally a 24/7 operating hours. Then coordinate with that station (BOS, in this example) to see if they have enough manpower and gates available for the arrival of your flight. Once checked, you can work a planned-diversion, land in BOS station and clear Customs there. This will turn your BOS-JFK portion of your flight to a domestic flight. Now, you can continue to JFK with almost no restriction. I say almost, because you still need to check with JFK to ensure they have manpower to unload the flight, clean, etc. that late in the day. If yes, then you are in good shape.

You also need to check all your airport/aircraft performance data to ensure you are safe to land/re-depart to and from there (BOS in this example).

There is always one last thing to check before executing this plan. And this is by far, one issue that might burn you from time to time and that is your Crew Legality.

Always check your crew legality before executing your plan. If you run out of crew time while on the ground in BOS station to clear Customs, then you either have to RON in BOS and cause the same problems that will be explained later, in KEF station or cancel the flight all together and protect your customers through different methods. This causes a lot of customer discomfort and operational disruption as you still need to move the airplane to the final destination to use it for next day's operation.

You always need to check with crew coordinators/schedulers and your managers to ensure you divert to a station where you ideally have unlimited CBP hours, crew reserves (When we say crew reserve, we basically mean either you have standby crew there to replace your original crew or you can easily move a new set of crew there to replace your original crew and continue) and/or customer protection options, (e.g., connecting flights, other means of transportation, hotels and etc). Diverting to a station where there's not a whole lot of connecting options, is probably not the best plan, from the crew and customers' prospective.

And as always, check with your lead dispatcher and managers to ensure they are in the loop, on board with the plan and support you along the way. They also can act as your DRM resources when you need some extra help especially with some coordination.

Remember: This is just a plan! The actual operation may not go according to your plan.

Crew may call fatigue, the mechanical issue lingers longer than expected, station cannot handle during your planned hours and etc.

You should always have some backup plans in case one of these items doesn't work as planned.

Most of the time, your next best option is to RON and continue to your final destination, the next day.

The reason for this is, regardless of the situation, you still need to bring the aircraft and crew back to where they belong. You might as well bring your customers, their luggage and other freight items (if any) on that same flight.

Always check with the following roles first: (In any order that makes sense operationally)

- Departure station
- Destination station
- Intermediate station
- Crew coordinator/scheduler
- Your lead dispatcher/manager

To Delay Overnight (RON)

Your second option is to delay the flight extensively so that your arrival time falls within CBP's operating hours (the next day). In airline industry terms, we call this extensive delay RON (Remain Over Night). This option should not be deemed your go-to option (unless combined with further issues) because it causes further complications including:

- You will lose the airplane that is needed for the next day morning's operation out of JFK airport. Now, you have to be on a lookout for a different airplane to protect next day's flight.

- You will have an airplane full of unhappy customers who have to come back again to the airport the next day and delay all their plans for another day.

- The KEF station should make hotel reservations for all those delayed customers and work on issuing new boarding passes for the next day's flight. Remember: Their current boarding passes are only good for that day. The next day's operation, even though the flight number may remain the same, is a different day, hence a new boarding pass must be issued for the customers to be able to pass through security and come back to the gate, the next day.

- You must also check the security of the KEF station to see if the station is safe for RON-ing your flight, in terms of aircraft and crew safety and security (Some airports are only deemed safe to operate during daylight hours and are not suitable for overnight stops).

- You should also always check with both departure and destination stations when setting up tomorrow's Estimated Time of Departure (ETD) to ensure they have airport slots, staffing and gate availability for that flight the next day. This will force both stations to pay overtime to bring their staff to work the flight on their time off (Once again, this is not a big expense compared to everything else, but still counts).

You (or your company's representative — in this case, the KEF airport team) have to apply for a new airport slot for the next day's operation. It can be much more difficult to get approval at an airport under very strict slot rules.

To Cancel the Flight

To cancel the flight and rebook the passengers on the next available flights because you cannot bring the flight during CBP hours. (Yes, it sounds ridiculous, and please don't bring it up as an option to your dispatch managers - unless the CBP issue is combined with some other issues that further complicate the case, e.g., crew legalities, aircraft not being ready mechanically and so on).

This option should always be considered as a last resort and be used only when all else has failed. Canceling a flight can cause disruptions for customers and the overall flight operation as it requires movement of an empty airplane and the crew and/or cancelling the next day's flight to balance.

When canceling in an out station, you are going to lose that airplane for the next day's operation. In this case, if you cancel your flight in KEF, you will not be short an airplane in JFK for the next day's operation. As a result, you may need to cancel the next day's flight from JFK to KEF, and operate the next day's KEF-JFK instead. This technique is called "Balancing".

Intentionally Left Blank

SCENARIO 2

Fuel Shortage (Due to Fuel Availability, Truck Driver Shortage, Infrastructure Issues and So Forth)

Fuel shortage is something that can happen for several different reasons. Some examples would be when fuel supply cannot reach a station due to a technical issue from the supplier, truck/driver shortage, pipeline technical issues and so forth.

The shortage can be as bad as no fuel left in the station for departing flights or just enough to support their departure out of that airport, so that they can land in a different station, get full gas required and continue to the final destination.

In a sense, it resembles the case of CBP limited hours where you had to have a planned diversion to clear Customs and continue to your final destination.

In this case, you need to land in a middle airport to get more fuel and then continue. Seems very straightforward, right? Not quite.

In order to make a fuel stop in an intermediate airport, you first need to ensure they have enough fuel to support their own flight in addition to your diverted flight.

Also, check if they have enough manpower and space to accept your flight. The last thing you want in a diverted airport is to have an airplane full of customers sitting on the ramp for an extended period of time waiting for the fuelers to fuel your flight and worst case, for the crew to time out. In scenarios like this, prior coordination is a must.

Always reach out to your manager to check and see if this is the option they want to use. They might have some other concerns for your flight, or even a different airport in mind for a refuel. They, after all, see the bigger picture as they are involved with several different flights. A simple check goes a long way and will save you so much time, believe me on that.

Next, you need to check your crew time. If your crew is super limited on their duty/flight time, you may need to coordinate a replacement crew to operate your flight out of the intermediate station.

Furthermore, you should check all the WX minimums, NOTAMs and performance restrictions of the intermediate airport to ensure you can land/re-depart from the intermediate airport. One other thing you need to check in this section is to ensure the airport you are planning to refuel in, is on your company's approved list of airports for that type of operation. (This is probably the first thing you need to check before everything else. If your company isn't authorized for a specific type of operation in that airport, you cannot plan on using that airport. For instance, if the intermediate airport is authorized only for a charter operation and not fueling, then a fueling operation should not be planned in there. Plus, if this intermediate airport is authorized as an alternate, you cannot plan it as a destination.)

It is always a good idea to check the customer protection and maintenance capabilities of your intermediate airport to plan for the worst-case scenario. Fueling scenarios go smoothly 99% of the time. The 1% would be for the situation you land in the airport and find out that there's a mechanical issue encountered during the flight that needs to be fixed before departure out of that airport.

If you cannot fix that problem before the crew times out, you may end up delaying/RON-ing your flight and then you would need some sort of accommodation for the customers and crew.

Under the circumstances that your airplane fix requires multiple days before it can fly again and customer protection is not possible, then you may want to consider setting up a **rescue flight**.

Rescue Flight

A rescue flight is a flight, usually from the original destination station (or any other station that has an additional and unassigned aircraft and crew that could be utilized — in reasonable distance) that goes to the intermediate airport empty (most of the time, unless there is a customer demand to open the flight for revenue) and brings the customers from the diverted flight to their final destination. The broken aircraft and original flight crew can stay there until the aircraft gets fixed and be able to fly to its original destination.

Intentionally Left Blank

SCENARIO 3

Severe Weather Events

Planning Phase

The good thing about these type of weather events is that you will have some time to plan and execute before they actually happen.

Of all severe weather events, thunderstorms and, consequently, hail can be very tricky specifically during the time of the year that the temperature and moisture levels are high causing pop-up heavy thunderstorms. They sneak up on you for a very short period of time (hopefully shorter than longer) and cause a lot of disruption to your operation depending on where they actually happen.

The worst-case scenario is when they happen right on the field during a busy hour (In airline industry, we call these peak hours when you have the highest number of departures or arrivals as "banks" — hence, arrival bank and departure bank).

To manage the flow of operation, Air Traffic Control has introduced a number of flow management initiatives and two of its most common ones are a ground stop (GS) and ground delay program (GDP).

In the simplest words, a ground stop is similar to hitting the pause button on your player device and to stop the music temporarily. As soon as you hit the play button again, the flow of music goes back to normal.

A Ground Delay Program (GDP) is when you put the music on slow motion. So, we intentionally slow down the flow to be able to manage it more effectively.

When a weather event happens (mostly in form of a thunderstorm), it restricts the ceiling and visibility needed for landing, brings hail damage, high wind speeds that exceed your aircraft performance capability and all of that equates to ATC only being able to handle a certain number of flights in each hour, if only it is safe to do so.

When it is not safe to bring in the flights to the airport because of all aforementioned hazards, then ATC puts your flight in airborne holding and it makes operational sense to divert the flight.

Airlines can also request from the ATC to put a customized initiative in place for a specific airport for their airline due to operational constraints.

So, you as a dispatcher, should proactively anticipate these types of operational constraints hopefully well ahead of time (based on your weather information) and account for more holding fuel. If you don't plan for it, then when your flight encounters the situation that requires airborne holding, they will choose to divert to another airport because of their fuel concerns.

Diverting to another airport means more work for you, your flight crew, your diversion airport, and misconnections for your customers.

Sometimes, regardless of all your hold fuel planning, your flight crew may divert based on the information they receive from the ATC.

When they do divert, they tend to divert to stations that they are most familiar with and have better customer service and aircraft handling capabilities. This almost always includes your large stations.

In the planning phase of an event, it is a great practice to brief your captain about the situation and discuss the "fuel and alternate planning" decision. Things go much smoother and more according to your planning when you actually discuss your plans with your flight crew well ahead of time.

You can also discuss the contingency plans in case the first option doesn't work for them.

This alone, shows that you are in control and have a 360-degree understanding of the situation. Your crew will have confidence in your dispatching abilities and they'll do their best to execute the plans.

If you reach out to your crew for the first time when they are actually in the moment (holding or planning to divert), it may be too late. It is always better to stay ahead by communicating weather and traffic to keep your crew informed and modify the plan if necessary

In some smaller, regional airlines, dispatchers are not authorized to use the larger stations as an alternate. The mainline reserves the right to use the larger airports for their much larger aircraft and operation.

If you have moved into a larger mainline airline from a regional airline, one thing you should always keep in mind and try to get into the habit is to use mainline and regional alternates for flight planning purposes.

When a large weather event happens around a hub, the larger alternate stations around them get inundated with diversions which can exceed their capacity, because most of the flight crew and dispatchers think the same in that moment when they are making diversion decisions. (Or maybe too many of your colleagues planned the same station as their primary alternate.)

What most likely happens in these situations is that diverted flights end up being on the tarmac for an extended period of time due to unavailability of airport resources from gates and ramp crew to gate agents and fuelers. So, there's a big chance of violating the 3-hour (in the case of international flights, 4-hour) tarmac rule.

In reality, diverting to a larger alternate airport during a significant weather event is probably not the best decision.

On the other hand, because a lot of different airlines divert to the same airport, sometimes the smaller airlines with fewer flights get higher priority over your flights.

Flight Phase

This is where your creative thinking and communication skills come into the picture.

Working with your flight crew before they're being placed on an airborne holding is the key to success of your flights. Sending ACARS messages when they're enroute to the final destination is much better since they usually have more time for planning and discussing your plans in the flight deck. This becomes even more critical when you know some of your large stations are already at the capacity with other flights. Let your crew know why you think diverting to a different (smaller) station is a better idea.

Any field information that you can provide while they are enroute or on a holding pattern and ready to divert counts. For example, the airport capacity for which they are planning to divert, how they are looking staffing and fueling wise, the average handling time, what they should be expecting and so forth.

Giving them this information ahead of time along with suggestions you might have helps them make better decisions for the operation along with the customers and crew they have on board.

Time permitting, it would be an excellent idea to give the station a heads up before sending the flight there. This will go a long way, allowing them to have some time to prepare for your flight with staffing, fueling, etc.

Keep in mind, sometimes if a flight lands at a station late in the evening, there would be nobody at the station to handle your flight. Fuelers and station operation agents go home for the day since they do not have scheduled flights. Thus, calling the station manager and giving them advance notice will be a key to expedited handling at the station level.

Also, share the information with your fellow dispatchers. In other words, communicate and coordinate so they can avoid overloading a specific station with diversions.

If you are dispatching for a large airline and end up working a large weather event, keep in mind that a smaller station might have fewer resources, but time wise, your flight can be handled with higher priority.

When diversions are in progress and you all of a sudden find yourself in full diversion mode, there is still some time to control the situation and avoid overloading your diversion stations.

In order to successfully accomplish that, you need to maintain continuous situational awareness as follows:

In your flight following tool (map), whatever that tool maybe, activate the range rings where it centers the ring on your problem airport. See below picture:

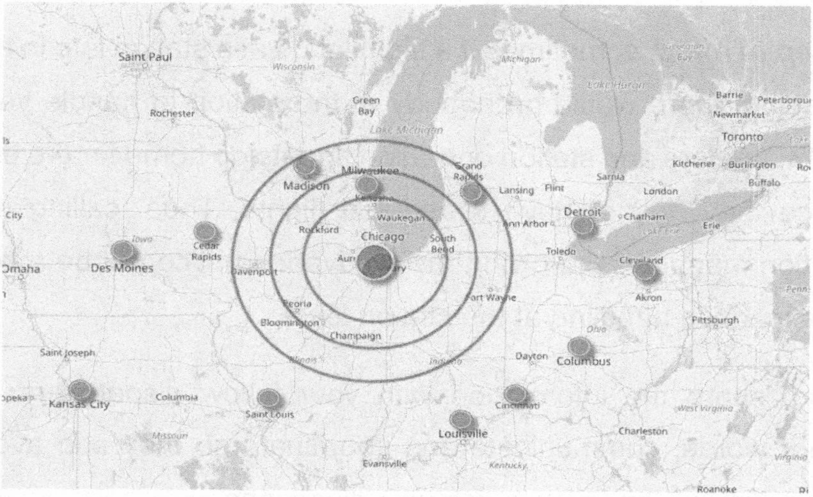

This way, you know exactly where your flights are located. Next, try to divide those rings into four quarters. These quarters usually represent your corner posts (or the entrance gateways to your airport).

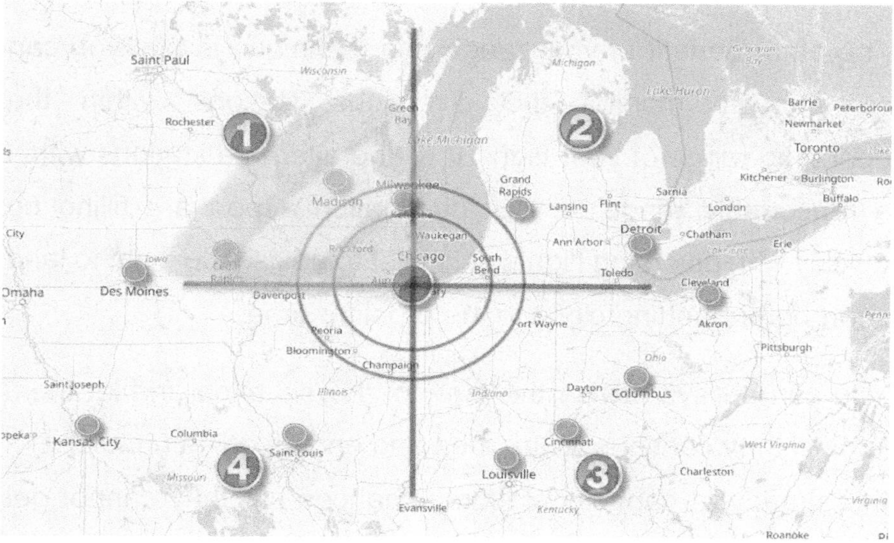

Locate the severe weather on the map to see what corner posts have been impacted by that weather. If there is a line of severe weather in a stretched solid line, ATC wouldn't allow your flights to use that corner post for arrivals and would want to reroute your flights around the weather using other corner posts.

Depending on the situation, your flight might not have enough fuel to accept that reroute. This is where a holding/diverting scenario comes up.

If the severe weather is a fast-moving cell that is going to clear your airport in a few minutes, holding will do it. If not, diversion is your option.

The other benefit to your range ring technique is that you can continuously monitor the diversions stations within the operating range of your flight. If all the alternate stations within a reasonable range of your destination airport are filling up quickly with diversion flights, it is best to advise the flight to land short before getting close to the problem area.

You can always advise the crew of the situation and let them know if they continue to the area and end up diverting to one of the already at capacity stations, chances are they cannot get handled and end up being on the ground for a much longer period of time, possibly in violation of the tarmac rule and/or crew legalities.

Diversion/On-the-Ground Phase

As mentioned in the previous section, being in continuous communication with your flight crew goes a long way and your crew feels they are being looked after and taken care of. Throughout the years, I have seen great feedback and recognitions coming from the pilots to thank their dispatchers for the great communication during an irregular operation.

Communicate with Your Flight Crew

Providing helpful information as stated in the *Flight Phase* section can also save you some time later once your flight is on the ground. It helps with unnecessary phone calls to ask you what to expect and etc. You will be very busy during a significant weather event, so if you can manage your communication effectively, it will save you precious time down the road.

Communicate with Your Managers

Once you get any useful information that you think your management team may find useful, pass that along. The information you can provide to your manager would include (but not necessarily limited to) the following:

- Contact Name plus their number in your diversion station.

- Is fuel readily available? If not, what is the expected availability time?

- Where are they trying to park your flight? Stairs, jet bridge, etc.

This also helps you avoid receiving extra phone calls from the managers asking for the status of your flight.

Please keep this in mind that as a dispatcher, you are considered a problem solver not a problem creator. If you are unable to come up with the best solution, always feel free to check with your lead dispatcher or manager, but let them know you have exhausted A, B and C options.

Park and Open the Door

Once your flight is on the ground, the clock is ticking. You want to make sure the airplane door has been opened and the customers are given the opportunity to deplane before the 3-hour mark (for domestic flights and 4-hour mark for international flights). If not, your company could be subject to a hefty fine.

You need to be in continuous communication with your diversion station operations staff to see what actions they are taking to gate or park your flight, open the door to let customers deplane (or at least be given the opportunity to do so) and fuel the aircraft for the next departure.

Communicate with Your Weight & Balance Team

During a large weather event, getting the latest passenger/bag information and sharing with your weight & balance teams will expedite your flight handling, as your flight needs the latest weight and balance information to re-depart from the diverted station. Make sure you verify with your station if anybody deplaned and/or was added during the time your flight was at the gate, etc. and if the total number of bags/amount of cargo has changed. You can always verify the information with your flight crew as well. Once you have that information, share it with your weight and balance team and have them finalize the flight and provide the performance information to the crew.

Communicate with your ATC Team

In order to expedite your flight handling, you need to check with the ATC and ask for priority handling. Depending on the size of your airline, you may have a dedicated team of coordinators that work specifically with the ATC. In this case, just reach out to them and communicate any limiting factors such as long onboard or crew legalities.

They should be able to give your flight a higher priority to depart and get back to the final destination when it is safe to do so.

Hurricane/Tornado/ATC Tower Evacuation/Airport Condition Concerns

When planning for a hurricane/tropical storm event, it is always advised to continuously check the track and outlook of the eye of hurricane/storm and know when it is expected to impact your operation.

If you are working for a large airline, there's a good chance that this task is being undertaken by other teams including the meteorology department and your operations managers.

If this task is usually assigned to you as a dispatcher, the following paragraphs help you form a mental checklist during these types of extreme weather events:

What needs to be checked is the amount of flooding and rain that this event is expected to bring and the maximum gust speeds and their direction (that helps with calculating the max crosswind component so you can decide if operating a flight during those hours is operationally possible).

The local station manager should always be looped in to get an update on the station's capabilities, local ATC and airport infrastructure availability, etc.

Things you want to consider during these type of extreme weather events are as follows:

- Are you able to operate your flight based on the maximum gust speed and wind direction?

- Is your braking action within the limits of your aircraft's performance?

- Can local employees/ATC tower controllers/fuelers come to work during that time?

- Are roads to the airport in good condition and open to public?

- Can customers come to the airport?

If the flooding/wind conditions exceed a normal level, you might even lose some of your airport infrastructure.

Safety is always your primary goal. You should not operate in an unsafe condition.

One last thing you need to coordinate is that to move your on-the-ground aircraft out of the station during the impact hours. Extreme wind and possibly hail will damage your aircraft and it will take your aircraft out of service for hours, if not days and weeks.

Intentionally Left Blank

SCENARIO 4

Overweight International Flight, Over by 20+ Passengers

With No Customer Protection

In this scenario, your fleet/network planning department has assigned a limited performance narrow-body aircraft to an international destination. This fleet assignment is based on the market demand and not necessarily a performance limitation.

As an airline, you do not want to provide too many seats to a market where you know you don't have much demand.

Remember, your aircraft seats are your airline's products. When supply exceeds demand, the prices are going down and vice versa.

When choosing to cater to a specific market with a limited-performance/seat aircraft, you are always on the edge of sacrificing revenue for the performance.

Below, we will bring some examples that can further restrict your flight from taking the planned payload.

Example 1- Alternate Restriction

When a nearby alternate airport becomes unusable for planning purposes, you are required to pick a different airport (in this case, a more distant one). A more distant airport means you'll likely need to carry more fuel. Consequently, you wouldn't be able to carry as much payload as you planned (Payload = Customers, bags and freight).

Example 2 – MEL-CDL

MEL/CDL items can lead to performance limitations or additional fuel requirement.

Example 3 – OTS Navaid

Another example is when a certain route becomes unavailable due to weather constraints, Out-Of-Service (OTS) Navaid and so on. This leads to selecting a route that is longer than the primary route. This also means carrying more fuel and hence less payload.

Example 4 – Runway Conditions

Yet another classic example of performance-limiting operation is runway crane operation, construction or maybe just a wet runway that requires a lighter airplane to operate. Lighter aircraft means less payload to take.

Example 5 – Wind Condition

Strong headwinds can sometimes result in 30+ minutes more in flying time and will cause the need for more fuel.

All above examples almost always lead to a serious concern and that is cutting the revenue. The problem becomes more complicated when you cannot protect customers for the next several days due to performance and weather limitations.

In this case, you'd always ask two questions: Should we stop for more gas and take on all the customers? or should we go direct instead and leave some customers behind?

Going direct means you'd take the full fuel load needed to operate a direct flight and consequently, leave some customers and/or bags behind.

Making a fuel stop means you are risking the crew timing out, customer misconnections and extra workload for your middle station where you stop to get fuel.

In order to make an educated decision, you need to work with a number of operational departments. More specifically, the weight and balance department (W&BD) if you have one, customer service department and of course, all three involved stations (departure, intermediate and final destination).

- *Weight & Balance Department:*

If your airline operates with a separate weight and balance department, always check with them first. The common practice to avoid an overweight situation is for W&BD to leave a spread of 1,000 to 2,000 lbs. of weight as a backup to ensure the actual payloads do not exceed the maximum weights. (More on this in my other book.)

In situations like this, you may want to check with your weight and balance agent and ask them to give you the maximum buffer weight gap for your planning purposes.

Also, having an accurate child count helps with weight calculation since children only weigh half of an adult for weight and balance purposes (check with your airline first! This is just for the sake of example here.).

- *Customer Service Department:*

It is always a good idea to ask for help from your customer service team. You are, after all, in the business of safely transporting customers, their luggage and goods. Having them on your side when making an operational decision will significantly help you.

Reach out to them (Customer Service Team) to verify if there is any way they can rebook some of the customers on the next available flights to help with the overweight situation.

If the customer protection on other flights is available, then involving them early on will ensure a smooth operation.

If this option is not available and there would be no protection for customers on the same day (and even the next few days), then a fuel stop may become your primary option.

- *Stations*:

It is easy to forget about all your involved stations when you are in the heat of the moment and doing all the behind-the-scenes planning.

The stations are those who implement your planning and always need to be kept in the loop. A simple communication goes a really long way. They are the ones facing your customers and when you keep them in the know, they can inform the customers of your plans. Studies show that when customers know ahead of time what an airline does, the complaint rates fall sharply.

To be more specific, you need to coordinate your plans with departure station so they can prepare to get volunteers to come off that flight and preferably protect them on a different flight. That task alone takes a long time and requires a lot of negotiations with customers. So, the sooner you inform them, the better they can plan their flight and get volunteers you need to fly a different flight.

If getting volunteers is not an option, due to lack of customer protection, etc., then you need to coordinate an enroute landing to get fuel and possibly a crew change. Also, check with your intermediate fuel station so they are ready for your flight, have a gate available for you, to line up their manpower to work the jet bridge, open the aircraft door, etc. They also need to check with the fueling department to have their fuelers on standby for your flight when it arrives to the gate/pad.

If you know your originating crew will not have enough time to operate the continuation of the flight out of your intermediate station, you need to coordinate with your crew scheduling team to dispatch a new crew to your flight. The intermediate station needs to know who is going to be replaced and when they will be arriving to the gate. If your aircraft is parked at a remote location, your current and new crew need to be transported to and from the terminal area.

As you can see, the intermediate station also needs to coordinate with a lot of different departments.

And last, but by no means least, your final destination station needs to know the new estimated time of arrival (ETA), the status of your flight and if it needs to clear Customs (in case of an international flight). They also need to provide an available gate, have the teams ready to accept the flight, connect the bridge, open the door, offload the bags, clean the flight, cater and fuel the aircraft and make it ready for the next flight. They are under a strict time pressure called minimum objective ground time (MOGT). That's how airports work. They live by their gates.

The better they can utilize their gate space, the more flights they can handle in any given time. When you're thinking airports, always think their gate space. They need to do all they can to avoid congestion on the ramp and at the gate level. As a result, your effective communication helps them plan their gates more efficiently.

Intentionally Left Blank

SCENARIO 5

HOT/HIGH Airport with Sudden Wind/Temperature Change, Overweight, Fuel Stop

Planning Phase

During your flight dispatcher certification course, it was thoroughly explained that a combination of hot and high airport is not ideal for a flight operation as the aircraft performance decreases significantly.

As the aircraft performance decreases, its ability to carry the payload also decreases. That means you wouldn't be able to carry all the customers, bags and freight that you'd normally carry in a non-high/hot airport and go non-stop.

As you're dispatching flights, you'd quickly learn about your usual suspects. In the U.S., Phoenix (PHX), Las Vegas (LAS) and Reno (RNO) are a few examples with airport conditions that are conducive to aircraft performance degradation.

Usually, the flights that are operating during early and late hours are not impacted that much since the temperature is normally cooler during those early or late hours compared to mid-day hours. Also, modern aircraft have higher engine performance capabilities that are designed specifically to operate out of airports with hot/high conditions.

For planning purposes, when operating out of these types of airports, you need to ensure you have temperature table/hours on your radar screen and plan for the worst-case scenario.

As an example, if operating out PHX at 10 a.m. with temperatures at 32 degrees Celsius requires five customers to be removed from the flight, it is a good practice to check 34 and 36 degrees Celsius as well to see how many more customers need to be removed should the temperature changes significantly.

Just for the sake of example, let's say you have to remove 20 customers for the flight to be able to operate within those temperature limitations.

Before jumping into any action, you need to check a few things:

- Check with your weight and balance agent. Are there any children on the flight that you can account for and adjust the weights?

- Can you plan for a closer alternate to the final destination that requires less alternate fuel?

- How's your final destination weather looking? Can you go alternate-none today?

- Can you use a higher performance engine bump to save the day without removing any customers? (Remember bumping engine performance increases the engine fatigue and wear and tear significantly and should only be used when all other options are exhausted.)

- Check with your customer service team to see if you end up removing 20 customers, would they have the capability to protect all those customers on next available flights? (Remember, removing customers voluntarily or involuntarily costs your airline money. So, if you can find a way to avoid that, you should use your due diligence to do so). The sooner you can communicate this with your airport team, the earlier they can find the volunteers willing to give up their seats on that flight.

If none of those considerations work with your particular flight, you may need to consider a planned fuel stop. This will help you take significantly less fuel so that you can carry the payload instead. And then land at an airport which doesn't have such restrictions to get the rest of required fuel for the continuation of your flight.

Flight Phase

When a planned fuel stop becomes the way to go, then you need to check with your diversion station to ensure they have the resources to promptly handle your flight.

You also need to check with your crew scheduling team to ensure your crew has enough duty/flight time left to operate the continuing flight out of the fuel stop station.

Arrival/On the Ground Phase

Once on the ground in your intermediate station, you need to make sure your flight is being handled as soon as operationally possible to avoid any long-onboard situations.

Depending on station's capabilities and resources, your flight may be parked at a remote pad to be fueled. This will require additional ground support.

Monitoring your crew times ensures you'll have a smooth operation and avoid last minute surprises.

Also, before posting the new ETD for your diversion flight, always check with your diversion (fuel stop) station to ensure you post a realistic ETD.

Intentionally Left Blank

SCENARIO 6

Runway Hard Closure, Slotted Airport, Crew Legalities Situation

When dispatching international flights for a large airline, always check the airport slots.

Think of airport slots as an appointment you are given by your doctor or for your car maintenance, etc. Unlike some of your ordinary appointments, airport slots are very strict. Violate them a few times, and you might lose your spot in that airport and get fined.

By violating, we mean arriving or departing earlier or later than your scheduled departure or arrival time.

Slotted airports are expecting you to operate on time and when you don't, they have means to enforce that.

One of the scenarios that recently came up was operating FROM (AAA) TO (BBB) a slotted airport. The destination airport (BBB) also had a NOTAM-published runway hard closure. The runway hard closure was scheduled close to the departure time of the returning flight (BBB back to AAA flight).

As you can imagine, departing late from AAA airport will cause a late arrival to BBB airport, and that increases the risk of operating within the runway closure hours from the BBB airport, which is not possible.

The situation gets even more complicated when you are using a set of crews that operates both legs. Any delay from the beginning to the end will jeopardize the crew legality and risk lengthy delays and possibly a flight cancellation.

In order to avoid this situation, you need to coordinate and check with the following teams:

- AAA Station
- Maintenance
- Crew scheduling
- ATC
- Dispatch lead/manager
- BBB station
- Customer service

AAA Station

Coordination with your departure station plays an instrumental role in operating a successful operation.

On time handling of your flight is critical for scenarios like this. The departure station needs to clean, fuel, cater, load and board the flight on time.

Flights like these should always get higher priority than other ones since any minor hiccups could have cascading effects on the overall operation of that flight. This definitely needs to be communicated and reminded to your AAA station.

What AAA can also do is to expedite crew movement depending on where the crew for that flight is coming from. More on this under the crew scheduling section.

Do everything you can to operate the flight out of your AAA station on-time.

Remember: In airline industry, if you are early, you are on time. If you are on-time, you are late!

Maintenance

Check with your maintenance department to ensure the aircraft assigned to this flight is clean and without any flight-restricting MELs. You cannot afford finding out about maintenance issues on this aircraft at or close to departure time.

Even a minor maintenance issue requires a long time to fill out and complete the logbook entry.

Always ask your maintenance team to show the aircraft OTS (Out of Service) and post an estimate time of repair (ETR) should the aircraft need to be fixed for anything.

If you do not have any ETR for that aircraft, then you are operating in complete darkness. You'd never know when you can actually count on this aircraft to come back in service and become operational. As a result, you wouldn't know if your crew would still be legal for a round trip operation or not. You wouldn't know if you'd be in compliance with airport slots or not. You wouldn't even know if you can return without violating the BBB airport runway hard closure.

You need to be on the top of your game with maintenance. If the aircraft is not READILY available to operate, it needs to be shown OTS with an ETR (Estimated Time of Repair).

Crew Scheduling

It is critical to check with crew scheduling to find out where your crew is coming from. If they are coming from home/hotel, then you need to inform AAA station to expedite their arrival to the gate.

If they are deadheading on a different flight, you absolutely need to be in close contact with the dispatcher of that flight. You also need to inform your ATC department (if your airline happens to have one) to ensure their flight receives expedited handling. If there's an ATC initiative active and your deadheading crew is stuck in that ATC initiative, you need to request for a "White Hat." This ATC term refers to exceptions requested by the airline to expedite one of their flights due to crew time, curfew, etc.

Also, if your crew has any legality concerns with their duty hours, always conference call with your crew scheduling department to ensure everyone is on the same page. Always stay on those calls to understand the limitations of your crew legality.

Air Traffic Control (ATC)

As mentioned above, communication with ATC is essential for the success of your mission.

Aside from the situation stated above regarding your deadheading crew, you also need to ensure the departure flight out of AAA station doesn't get caught in any ATC initiative. Always request for a white hat should you need to.

One other important subject to check with ATC is to ensure your flight doesn't get last minute re-route that requires more fuel and extended time to fly. Remember, a longer route increases the flight time that you cannot afford to have. Also, in case the onboard fuel is not sufficient for your trip, your flight needs to come back to the gate and get more fuel. All that, requires more time, that you don't have!

Dispatch lead/manager

Since these types of flights are time critical, always check with your dispatch lead/manager to use a higher cost Index to speed up your flight. Even a few minutes gained in the air helps your crew and BBB station to successfully operate your return flight.

Sometimes, even with all the preparation and coordination, things happen beyond your control and your flight gets delayed beyond the operating hours. This situation leaves you with a few options.

- To operate the flight from AAA station and RON in BBB station and operate the return flight on the next day.
- To RON in AAA station and operate the flight to BBB station the next day.
- Cancel the round-trip flight, protect your customers on other flights and start fresh the next day.

These are some of the decisions that your lead or manager usually makes (due to their economical nature), so always check with them before taking any further action here.

Customer Service

It is always the best practice to follow up with your customer service team. You are in the business of transporting customers (passengers and their bags, mail, freight or combination of all three) safely from point A to point B. You definitely need to keep your customers on your radar screen at all times. Your decisions and actions directly impact them.

Check with your customer service team to see if they would be able to protect all customers preferably on your own flights (if not, then partner airlines). If the answer is no, then you may want to consider up-gauging (in other words, use a larger airplane that can hold more passengers and bags/cargo) your next-day flight so you can accommodate more customers.

SCENARIO 7

Cancel Vs. RON

The cancellation versus Remain Over Night (RON) decision can always be a tough one since it impacts a lot of people, from customers to crew to airport staff.

We generally cancel a flight when the resources (aircraft, crew, airport slots, etc.) become unavailable or the time they become available exceeds beyond the reasonable operational time period. What do we mean by that?

You are working an international flight 234 LAX-AMS ETD 1800z. Normally this is a 13-hour flight (for the sake of easy calculations), so the ETA in AMS will be 0700z. (the next day)

30 minutes prior the departure, you are made aware that the ACARS system is not working and your aircraft will be taken out of service (OTS). Your maintenance crew informs you that the task needs 11 hours to finish and you do not have any other aircraft that you can swap to and continue.

What is obvious is that your crew will not be legal to operate this flight. You cannot hold your customers at the terminal for 11 hours until the aircraft is ready to go. You also don't want to exhaust all your departure airport staff at the gate until the aircraft comes back to service. So, what is the right thing to do?

Well, you may say, the easiest thing to do is to put the crew in bed and customers back home/hotel (RON) and bring them back when the aircraft comes back in service. Right? Not always!

Delaying an international flight like this that crosses multiple time zones, is not always the best option. Depending on how much ground time you might have in AMS, the crew availability in AMS for the return flight, slot assignment, staff availability in AMS and so forth, RON-ing the flight wouldn't seem like a good option. If the flight crew is the one that needs to bring the flight back to LAX, they need to get their minimum required rest period before they can operate the flight back to LAX. And because AMS is ahead of LAX time-wise, you may end up losing your aircraft for multiple days before you can have it back in LAX.

In this case, canceling your round-trip flight seems to be a better option. You will have your resources available to you without losing them for multiple days. Also, your customer service teams can protect your current customer booked on this flight much better once a flight is canceled. They usually have access to multiple airlines/flights on which they can protect your customers.

Sometimes however, RON-ing the flight is not a bad idea either.

RON-ing a flight usually makes more sense when you do not have enough resources to protect your customers on. In other words, you (as an airline) cannot book your customers on a different flight (either your own or your partner flights).

For example, your flight has been taken OTS in an outstation (any station other than a big hub) at 1900 local time with an estimated time of repair set for 0500 the next day.

As you can see, in a small station (or sometimes, depending on the time of the day, in a larger hub too), your remaining flight options disappear rather quickly. You basically do not have any other flights left to take your customers where they needed to be. Also, your aircraft, when it returns back in service, needs to go back to where it belongs (e.g., your hub station).

In this case, it doesn't make sense to cancel your flight because you technically cannot protect your customers on any other flight. You might as well delay your flight overnight (RON) until it comes back in service and then take your customers with you to the hub station in the morning, where they have a lot of connection options (if the hub station is not their final destination).

As you could clearly see in the aforementioned examples, cancel or RON decisions should be made on a case-by-case basis and there's no one-size-fits-all approach to that.

Intentionally Left Blank

SCENARIO 8

Security Event at the Terminal (Suspicious Bag, Car, Etc.)

After the 9/11 tragedy, airport and airline security measures have intensified exponentially. Any unattended bag, vehicle or suspicious activity on airport premises is being looked at as a threat to aviation and is being treated as such.

You might have seen this in person or on the news that threats like this usually result in area evacuation, bomb threat teams attending the scene and so on.

If threats like this happen outside of the terminal area, in the streets ending to the airport or off-premise in general, it may cause some transportation traffic. Remember, if you have crew coming from home or hotel to the terminal, they might get impacted by this traffic and be tardy for their departure.

You usually get this kind of information from your local airport team. When receiving calls like this, always ask them about the extent of this event, how long is the wait time, what flight departures they have and if they need an adjustment to the departure time (ETD adjustment).

If this event happens inside the terminal, depending where it is, it might impact different phases of your operation.

Inside the terminal at the ticket counter area:

If this is the case, you might lose your ticket counter operation and security checkpoints adjacent to them for a period of time.

If this happens during a busy bank, you might end up delaying a lot of your departing flights, because you will end up having a lot of unchecked customers, who are going to miss their flights unless their departing flight gets delayed from their current departure point.

You also need to check with your customer service teams to see how many customers will misconnect because of that delay.

Based on the standard operating procedure of your airline, you may need to use a higher cost index (refer to my book on this subject) to speed up your flight to shave off some of that delay in the air.

You may also need to inform your destination airport so that they can park your flight closer to the connecting flight to transfer the customers as soon as they land and deplane the arriving flight.

Also, checking with the dispatcher who is working the connecting flight and informing them about the possible misconnection situation will be an amazing customer service.

Inside the secure area/at the gate

If this is where your security event happens, there's a good chance flights at the gate and ready to depart will be impacted.

If the extent of evacuation goes beyond your gate and ends up sending customers outside of the secure area, they need to be re-screened for departure and that leads to extensive departure delays.

If you have flights in the air or on approach to the airport, once again depending of the extent of this event, you may need to have your flight parked at a remote location or even diverted to an alternate airport to avoid the destination airport all together until the situation is resolved.

This will lead to disruption of operation and needs to be coordinated with different teams to minimize the impact.

- Check with your crew scheduling team to ensure your crew has enough time to continue to the final destination once the issue is resolved.

- Check with the station to ensure they send you and your managers updates as they become available.

- Check with your diversion station to have gate, staff and fuelers on standby for expedited handling.

- Inform your managers (time permitting).

Inside the Baggage Screening Area (Checked Bag Screening)

If the security happens in the baggage screening section of your departure airport, then most likely it will impact your departure flight. Depending on how many bags are being impacted, you may need to delay your flight to ensure these bags make it to the flight.

You may also need to check with the following teams to ensure the impact is minimized:

- Airport operations to see how many bags are impacted.
- Customer service team to see if bags could be loaded on the next flight.
- Weight and balance department to see if they can handle the excess bags on the next flight.
- Crew scheduling to ensure any delay will not impact the operation and crew legalities.

SCENARIO 9

Operating In and Out of Airports with Strict Curfew Hours

(SAN/AMS/DCA/LGA)

Curfews are the times of the day that the city does not accept your flight to land or depart in and outside of their airport. This is mainly due to noise abatement and they are either based on the fixed hours (like SAN airport) or aircraft type/weight restrictions (DCA airport).

The way these airports enforce curfew is to fine the operator (airline) every time they violate this curfew. Sometimes, the issue is not the fine that your airline has to pay, but the risk of losing the landing/departure rights should the violation continue.

In order to avoid that, dispatchers should be very careful if their flights get delayed mainly due to weather, maintenance and or crew legalities.

Once again, we divide this section into three phases as following:

Flight Planning, Flight, Post Flight

Flight Planning

Not everything goes according to your planning all the time and this becomes a potential issue when operating in and out of an airport with strict curfew hours.

Things that usually go wrong during planning phase are as following:

- *Maintenance*

When ready to operate a time-sensitive flight that is scheduled to arrive closer to your destination airport curfew hours, you need to be extra cautious with your aircraft being in good shape to operate the flight. Any minor delay may end up falling outside of curfew hours and risk your flight getting significantly delayed or even canceled.

To avoid that, you need to check with your maintenance team to ensure the aircraft you'll be using for your flight is in full operating condition and there are no restricting MELs that limit your operation. No icing condition MELs are one of the few examples that might restrict you from going to the specific airport.

If you are made aware of a maintenance issue that could possibly impact the on-time performance of your flight, you may need to bring it up to your manager or whoever is responsible for aircraft swaps in your airline so, a speedy and proactive aircraft swap can be facilitated. This action preferably needs to be done two hours prior to your scheduled departure to avoid potential curfew violation. Two hours is usually the standard time based on how busy the departure station may be. The new aircraft needs to be cleaned, catered and fueled for your new mission, as well as loaded and finally boarded for your departure. Don't forget that your crew and customers need to go to the new gate as well. Most of these activities could be completed concurrently, so two-hour time frame leaves a good cushion for unforeseen, last-minute issues.

- *Weather and ATC Delays*

Weather and, consequently, the ATC initiatives that can cause delayed operations are some of the most important reasons you might miss your curfew hours.

Depending on where the weather is, and what type of ATC initiatives are in place, you might get delayed for hours.

Larger and busier airports live by their gate space. They need to handle your departure so they can work on arriving flights and future departing flights. So, having your flight delayed while at the gate is not their ideal situation.

Let's say you are working a CLT to DCA flight. Your destination airport, DCA, is experiencing some moderate thunderstorms expected to impact the terminal closer to your flight's arrival time. ATC has initiated a low-rate 1st and 2nd tier ground delay program. Your EDCT (Expected Departure Clearance Time - also known as wheels-up time) is for the next 70min.

CLT would like to push your flight off the gate, and have your flight wait for their departure turn while waiting on a taxiway or somewhere away from the gate so that they can handle some more flights while waiting for your departure.

You can help your flight by requesting a white hat since there is a chance you cannot land in DCA prior to curfew hours. Also, stay in close contact with your ATC department to ensure your flight doesn't get unreasonable re-routes that requires more fuel than they have onboard. If that becomes the case, your flight needs to go back to the gate (if there's one readily available, if not, they have to wait even longer for a gate), get more fuel and re-depart.

Going through all of that, you need to ensure you're still able to operate within legal operating hours and are not going to violate curfew hours.

- Crew Legalities

During normal operating hours, crew legality will not be an issue (most of the time). It (crew legality) will however become an issue when stuck in an ATC initiative and being pushed off the gate. Since the brakes have been released and your crew duty time clock is ticking, you are technically racing against the time to get them up in the air. There are a couple of restricting times you need to check (or have your crew scheduler check) at all times to ensure they are OK to fly.

To obtain the latest information on Crew Duty Time and other legalities, please check 14 CFR Part 117.

Flight

- *International Arrival Flights (AMS, etc.)*

If you gain some time in the air and your flight time decreases, due to a shorter route, excessive tailwind, etc., you may end up with an ETA that falls within curfew hours.

Events like these need to be coordinated well ahead of time with the destination airport to avoid hefty fines.

Depending on how much earlier your flight is set to arrive, you have a couple of options:

Before arriving to the final destination, your crew might be able to request ATC to place them on a holding pattern to arrive past curfew hours.

Another option would be to push on-time and wait on the ramp at departure station to gain some time before departure. This is perhaps a better of the two options because, you depart on time (at least push off the gate on time), burn the least amount of fuel on the ground, and leave the gate so they can use it to handle different flights, when needed.

Either way, make sure your managers are well aware of this situation. A slight ETD adjustment might be required that they can coordinate with your network planning department.

- *Domestic Arrival Flights (SAN, etc.)*

Violating a domestic curfew doesn't necessary mean paying a regular fine every time and moving on. Sometimes these fines grow exponentially depending on the number of violations. If your airline continuously arrives past the curfew hours, you risk losing the landing rights and facing significant fines. Diverting to a neighboring station would probably be a better idea to avoid all of the above.

Post-Flight

Before diverting to a neighboring station, you'll first need to check with them to see if they have resources to accept and handle your flight. What they need to be aware of is that your flight will not depart that night once landed. If the actual destination is within the driving distance from the diversion airport, your customer service team might be able to coordinate busses to move the customers and their bags to their final destination.

If the diversion station is not within reasonable driving distance, they should be accommodated in a hotel to depart in the morning.

Remember, you need to have your airplane and crew in your final destination for the next day's operation. So, either taking an empty flight with crew only and ferry that to the final destination, or an airplane with the original customers on. Either way you need to move the aircraft and crew to the final destination in the morning. That ferry flight segment needs to be coordinated with your destination airport to ensure they have gates available for your arrival in the morning hours.

SCENARIO 10

Passenger/Crew Medical Diversion

This is one of those scenarios that requires a lot of coordination between the dispatchers and pilots, dispatch management, maintenance, diversion station, final destination station and your customer service teams.

Imagine your flight is going from PHL to LHR on an A350 aircraft. Flying over the Atlantic Ocean, captain sends you a message that one of your customers or cabin crew members has symptoms similar to a heart attack.

The onboard doctor (one of the customers) and your on-the-ground physician recommend immediate diversion and captain is preparing to return back to the U.S. to take the ill customer or crew member to a hospital as soon as possible.

Since your flight is over the ocean, you'll have a few minutes to check a few options, so don't panic!

You need to check with the following people to come up with the best diversion station option:

- Your on-duty dispatch manager
- Maintenance
- Crew scheduling
- Diversion station
- Customer service team

We will expand on each and every one of them here shortly but before that, Remember:

You need to think outside-of-the-box here. Not always your closest airport is your best option! Your creativity and resourcefulness go a really long way.

On-Duty Dispatch Manager

Check with your on-duty manager, to know which station has more resources available for your flight.

Our scenario is about an ill customer or crew member and it doesn't necessarily end up being a maintenance issue, but you never know. Chances are an overweight landing causes some maintenance issues that need to be addressed before re-departure.

Use your duty manager as your DRM (Dispatch Resource Management) tool. Let them check some of the items for you while you focus more on the safety and operation of your flight.

Maintenance

Check with your maintenance team to see if they have the capability of handling and inspecting your overweight landing aircraft.

You probably don't want to divert your flight to a station that can only handle a narrow-body aircraft. Also, there are some strict oxygen bottle requirements onboard the flights that are part of your Minimum Equipment List (MEL).

You need to check with the maintenance team to ensure they either have your part readily available or can find it quickly for your flight to continue. Otherwise, you are technically unable to re-dispatch your flight without complying with the requirements of your aircraft MEL.

Crew Scheduling

Check with your crew scheduling team to know if your crew will have duty/flight time left to continue their flight after the customer/crew member deplane. If their time will be very limited upon landing, you might end up re-crewing the entire flight crew to be able to continue the flight.

Also, if the situation involves a crew member removal, chances are that you'll go below minimum required crew members and then once again, be unable to legally re-dispatch your flight. If that's the case, diverting to a station where you can have a reserve crew available would save the day.

Diversion Station

Check with your diversion station to ensure they have resources available to support your flight. In other words, check to see if they have the ability to safely park and to get customers off the aircraft through jet bridge, stairs, etc.

You definitely don't want to divert to a station without a tow bar for your aircraft or to a station without any available hotel rooms.

Word of advice: Always check the hotel availability. A very seasoned friend once said, *"these type of operations with limited crew times, almost always end up RON-ing inside the diversion station"*. So, make sure you have rooms to accommodate your customers, if the need arises.

Other things that need to be checked with your diversion station (depending on where that diversion station is located) are availability of Customs and acceptance of COVID test requirements (during 2021/2022 times — hopefully this won't be the case for the years to come). If you divert to a station that has some strict Customs and border laws and does not honor the COVID tests beyond their issuance date, then you'd dig yourself into a larger hole.

Customer Service

And last but by no means least, check with your customer service team to ensure you have enough backup to protect your customers in case things don't go as planned. If, for some reason, you lose your aircraft or crew for that flight, would your customer service team be able to book your customers on a different flight to their final destination? If not, it is better to divert to a station with better protection options.

All said, the nature of your emergency always dictates your decision. Sometimes you wouldn't have the luxury of extra time to check all that. All you can and need to do is to divert to the nearest suitable airport and provide the weather, and airport updates to your crew to land the flight and take care of their onboard emergency. ***Everything else will have a lower priority***.

Be aware: These types of events are usually being recorded by customers onboard, and because of their nature, they usually find their ways into the news. Just a heads up!

Made in United States
Orlando, FL
02 October 2024

52238134R00071